'81 08509

DATE DUE			

HOW DID WE FIND OUT
ABOUT OIL?

How Did We Find Out . . .?
Books by Isaac Asimov

HOW DID WE FIND OUT

ABOUT OIL?

Isaac Asimov
Illustrated by David Wool

WALKER AND COMPANY
New York

Library of Congress Cataloging in Publication Data

Asimov, Isaac, 1920-
How did we find out about oil?

(How did we find out . . . series)
Includes index.
SUMMARY: Describes the origin, composition, and
historical and modern uses of petroleum./
1. Petroleum—Juvenile literature. [1. Petroleum]
I. Wool, David. II. Title.
TN870.3.A84 1980 553.2'82 79-5448
ISBN 0-8027-6380-4
ISBN 0-8027-6381-2 lib. bdg.

First published in the United States of America
in 1980 by the Walker Publishing Company, Inc.

Published simultaneously in Canada by Beaverbooks,
Limited, Pickering, Ontario.

Trade ISBN: 0-8027-6380-4
Reinf. ISBN: 0-8027-6381-2

Library of Congress Catalog Card Number: 79-5448

Printed in the United States of America

10 9 8 7 6 5 4 3 2 1

To
Marilyn Infeld Kass
Donna Gassen
Barbara Coleman
the happy hypodermicists.

HOW DID WE FIND OUT . . . SERIES
Each of the books in this series on the history of
science emphasizes the process of discovery.

Contents

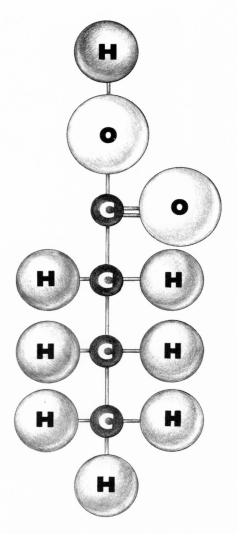

**A SMALL FATTY ACID MOLECULE—
THE TYPE OF BUILDING
BLOCK FOR A SIMPLE
FAT MOLECULE**

1 The Formation of Oil

MANY HUNDRED million years ago, simple living creatures existed in the ocean. As yet there were no fish, no sharks, no lobsters, but there were one-celled plants and animals in great numbers.

These one-celled organisms contained fats and oils just as we do. Fats and oils are made up of three kinds of atoms*: carbon, hydrogen, and oxygen.

A number of these atoms stick together to form a tiny structure called a "molecule" (MOL-uh-kyool). A molecule of fat or oil is built up out of a chain of carbon atoms. There can be short chains of as few as four carbon atoms or long chains of as many as twenty-four of them. Hydrogen atoms are attached to each carbon atom, and there are just about twice as many hydrogen atoms as carbon atoms. At one end of the chain there are two oxygen atoms.

If one small one-celled organism is eaten by another, the one that is eaten is digested. Its molecules are pulled apart, and the fragments are put together

*See *How Did We Find Out About Atoms?* Walker, 1976.

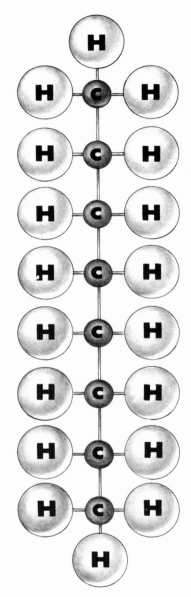

HYDROCARBON MOLECULE—OCTANE

again in a slightly different way. New fat molecules are formed.

Sometimes a one-celled organism dies without being eaten, but its remains are usually eaten afterward by some living thing or other.

For the most part, then, molecules are pulled apart and put together. Living things eat or are eaten; some come into existence; some die; but the same atoms are used over and over again.

When a cell dies and drifts down to a shallow sea bottom, it might become covered with sand before any other living thing can eat it and then it just stays there. In that case, the molecules still fall apart and go back together again, but more slowly. The changes take place because of heat or pressure or chemical action in the sand, but they are not the same changes that would take place if living things were involved.

One of the changes that takes place involves the fat molecules. The two oxygen atoms at one end of the molecule chain attach themselves elsewhere. The carbon chain is left behind with only the hydrogen atoms attached. The resulting substances, containing molecules made up only of carbon and hydrogen atoms, are called "hydrocarbons" (HY-droh-KAHR-bunz).

Some of the carbon chains break up so that there are molecules with only three carbon atoms, or only two, or even only one. Other carbon chains attach together and become unusually long.

There are also pieces of molecules that come from elsewhere than the original fats. There are rings of carbon atoms, for instance. Occasionally, there are also other kinds of atoms, such as those of nitrogen and sulfur. For the most part, though, the buried cells change into a very complicated mixture of large numbers of different kinds of hydrocarbon molecules.

The properties of the different hydrocarbon molecules depend partly on the length of the carbon chain. When a molecule contains only one to four carbon atoms, the substance they make up is a gas. If you had some of it in an open bottle, it would look just like air. It would drift out of the bottle and mix with the air.

Molecules with longer carbon chains, from five carbon atoms up, are liquids. If you had some of it in a bottle, it would look like water. (Of course, it wouldn't be water. It would smell differently, and it would behave differently.)

Such hydrocarbon liquids vaporize easily. That is, if you let them stand in a dish, they would dry up. The liquid would turn into a gas and would mix with the air. If the liquid were heated gently and carefully, it would vaporize more quickly.

The longer the carbon chain, the more slowly the liquid vaporizes, and the more it has to be heated before rapid vaporization takes place.

If a hydrocarbon liquid is heated, boiling begins to take place at a certain temperature. That is the "boiling point."

The longer the carbon chain, the higher the boiling point. For very short carbon chains, the boiling point is so low that even when the temperature is freezing, that temperature is high enough to boil the liquid. That's why hydrocarbon molecules with such short carbon chains are gases. They've already boiled.

Hydrocarbons with really long carbon chains aren't even liquid. They are soft, greasy solids, often black and sticky. If these soft solids are heated, they can be made to melt and become liquid.

If they are heated still more, you might think they would boil and become gases. Actually, though, very long carbon chains, if heated, tend to break up into shorter chains. The molecules "crack."

When one-celled living things turn into hydrocarbons under the sand and other rocky material that covers them, a complicated mixture is formed of gas and liquid and solid.

The mixture can be buried deeper and deeper under the sand and grit. The sand and grit that settles down is called "sediment" (SED-ih-ment) from a Latin word meaning "to settle." As this layer of sand and other material grows thicker and thicker, its own weight forces the bits of matter to stick together and form "sedimentary rock" (sed-ih-MEN-tuh-ree).

This rock forms under water, usually under shallow parts of the ocean near the shore. As many, many years pass, these bits of ocean bottom may slowly rise higher, and the ocean may drain away, leaving the sedimentary rock on dry land; but it still contains the hydrocarbon mixture.

Because the hydrocarbon mixture has an oily, greasy feel to the touch, it is called "oil." There are other oily feeling substances in plants and animals (think of olive oil or chicken fat). Since people had to distinguish between the different kinds of oil, the hydrocarbon mixture in the sedimentary rock was called "rock oil." (Of course, the rock oil was originally formed from the oil in living things, but this wasn't known at first.)

Instead of rock oil we can say "petroleum" (peh-TROH-lee-um), which is from Latin words meaning "rock oil."

These days, though, we usually just say "oil." Petroleum has become so important to us that when we say "oil" we know that's what we mean. We don't mean olive oil or chicken fat.

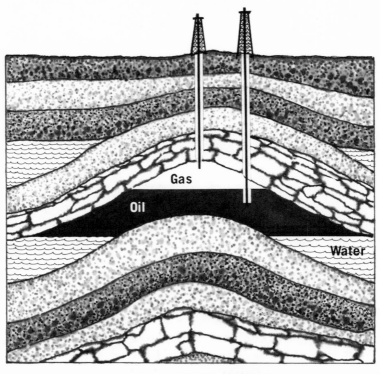

SEDIMENTARY ROCK SHOWING LOCATION OF OIL

2 The Early Uses of Oil

THE SEDIMENTARY rock in which petroleum is found was formed from bits of sand and grit so tiny that little air spaces still exist inside that rock. When the sedimentary rock is under water, water fills all those little air spaces.

Even when the sedimentary rock is on dry land, it is often quite a way below the surface, far enough down so that it is surrounded by water. (There is usually water somewhere below the surface of the ground. That is why people dig wells to get drinking water.) This means that even on dry land, the tiny air spaces in sedimentary rock can be filled with water.

Oil also collects in the tiny air spaces if it is present. Oil is lighter than water and floats on top of it. If more and more water soaks into the rock, the oil is slowly forced higher and higher. Finally, it is possible for the oil to reach the surface.

When the oil does that, the gases in the hydrocarbon mixture just drift away and mix with the air. The liquids vaporize, and the vapors mix with the air, too. Left behind is just a soft, sticky black solid.

17

Deposits of solid, left-over petroleum are common in the Middle East, around the Persian Gulf. This sticky black solid is known by several different names.

One of them is "asphalt" (AS-fawlt). There was so much of this material about the shores of the Dead Sea that the ancient Romans called it "Lake Asphaltites" (AS-fawl-TITE-eez).

Another name is "bitumen" (bih-TYOO-men); but the most frequently used name is "pitch."

The ancients who lived in the Middle East found uses for pitch. It was sticky; it wouldn't mix with water; it wouldn't allow water to soak through. If pitch were smeared on wooden objects, it would make them watertight for that reason.

Pitch was therefore very important in ship building. It would be placed between the planks used to build the ships and that would keep them from leaking.

This is mentioned in the Bible. When Noah is instructed to build an ark, God tells him to "pitch it within and without with pitch."

Then, too, when Moses was born, his mother had to hide him because Pharaoh had ordered all the male children of the Israelites killed. She therefore made a little boat out of bulrushes, a kind of reed.

She wove the reeds together, placed the child inside, and then let the small boat float down the river, hoping that some Egyptian would find it and rescue him. Of course, if the boat were just woven out of reeds, water would quickly soak through and it would sink. She therefore "daubed it with . . . pitch" to make it waterproof.

There were other ways of using the pitch. Ancient people had to irrigate their fields from nearby rivers.

BAGHDAD WICKER BOATS CAULKED WITH ASPHALT

This kept plants growing even when it didn't rain for a while. The water would be led through ditches, but those ditches would be of no use if they absorbed the water. The ancient Babylonians would line the ditches with sand or reeds that had been mixed with pitch. The pitch would make them waterproof.

The river banks would sometimes be built up high into "levees" so that when the rainy season came and the river level became high, the water would not spread out over the countryside. To build the levees, sand might be piled high; but the water might then soak through after a while. If pitch were added to the sand, it would not only make the sand stick together, it wouldn't allow the water to get through.

Pitch was also used as a sticky cement to hold bricks together, to hold metal blades to handles, to hold tiles to a wall, and so on.

This type of use for pitch went on right into modern times. When European navigators began to explore the world in the 1400's and 1500's, they found pitch in several places in the world.

Pitch was found in Cuba, in eastern Mexico, and along the western coast of South America. In about 1600, Sir Walter Raleigh discovered a whole lake of pitch in the island of Trinidad just north of South America.

Seepages of pitch were also found in the Indonesian islands and in the American colonies of New York and Pennsylvania.

All such finds were considered of great value, for the explorers used it to smear over the joints of their boats to prevent leaks—just as Noah was told to do to the ark.

Sometimes pitch was used as a medicine. The softer, more liquid parts could be smeared on sore places as a liniment. It may even have helped a bit. At least it would keep insects away.

Sometimes it was swallowed because it acted as a laxative. Even today this is sometimes done, though in modern times the petroleum is carefully refined. A pure, clear liquid is obtained from petroleum that is called "mineral oil."

Hydrocarbon molecules will combine with the oxygen of the air. In other words, they will burn.

The hydrogen atoms in the hydrocarbon molecule

PITCH LAKE IN TRINIDAD

will combine with oxygen to form water molecules. The carbon atoms will combine with oxygen to form carbon dioxide molecules.

The combination releases heat. The mixture of combining gases gets so hot that it gives off light and glows. The glowing mixture blows this way and that in currents of air and is what we call "fire."

When a hydrocarbon is a gas, it mixes freely with air and catches fire easily. It continues to burn easily.

Liquid hydrocarbons will burn in the same way if they give off vapors to begin with. The vapors mix with the air, and if they catch fire, they will burn. The heat of the burning warms the liquid and makes it give off more vapor and burn more rapidly.

The smaller the hydrocarbon molecules the more likely it is to give off vapors, or to be a gas to begin with, and so the more readily it will burn.

Indeed, hydrocarbons can burn too fast for comfort. The burning may suddenly become so fast that a great deal of gas or vapor will combine all at once and the result is an "explosion."

How did people find out that petroleum would burn?

Probably, they found out by accident. There were places in the Middle East where petroleum leaks at the surface gave off hydrocarbon gases. If someone had built a campfire near the place, he might have been startled when there was an explosion and a flame then shot up out of the ground.

What's more, the flame wouldn't go out. It would keep on burning.

This would surely strike everyone as very unusual. When an ordinary fire is built, it must be fed with fuel all the time or it will go out. How was it then that a flame came out of the ground and then kept on burning day after day after day without the addition of fuel?

It must have seemed like a miracle. Perhaps the story of the burning bush in the book of Exodus in the Bible arose from such a flame appearing.

The ancient Persians developed a religion in which such "eternal fires" played an important part. In fact, the ancient Persians were sometimes called "fire-worshippers" for that reason.

On the other hand, it is possible that some people were frightened by the eternal fires and thought them the product of demons. It may have made them think that somewhere under the earth there was a region of eternal fire and that every once in a while a bit of it leaked to the surface. That, and the experience of volcanoes (which also seemed to bring fire up from the depths of the earth), may have convinced people of the existence of an underground Hell where the spirits of the dead were tormented.

Sometimes one could obtain from pitchy deposits a clear liquid that burned easily. The Persians called it "neft," meaning "liquid," and the Greeks picked up the word and made it "naphtha" (NAF-thuh).

The ancients were used to liquids that burned, but usually these liquids came from living things. Vegetable oils could be burned in lamps, for instance. A piece of thick twine called a "wick" was floated on the oil; or else the oil was placed in a container with an upper opening to one side (like a small teapot), and the wick was led up the spout. The oil would soak up through the wick. When the wick was set on fire, the

ANCIENT OIL LAMP

heat of the fire would cause the oil to vaporize. The vapor would catch fire and make a flickering flame. More oil would soak up the wick and vaporize, and the flame would continue to burn until all the oil was gone.

The burning liquid from pitch, which behaved like oil from plants or animals, must have surprised people. It may have seemed as supernatural as the burning gases. Sometimes, therefore, it was used to feed holy flames—flames that burned to worship a god.

In the first chapter of the second book of Maccabees, a book written about events among the Jews in the second century B.C., there is a tale about the Second Temple being built. A search was made there for the sacred fire that used to burn in the original Temple of Solomon.

The searchers "had not found fire but thick liquid." The priests were ordered "to sprinkle the liquid on the wood." Later on, "a great fire blazed up so that all marveled." At the end of this first chapter, the liquid is identified as naphtha.

The semisolid portions of pitch could also sometimes be made to burn, though it did so slowly, smoldering rather than flaming. That had a use, too.

Generally, such fires smoked and smelled a great deal and were choking and unpleasant. Suppose such pitch were placed in a metal container in the middle of a room and allowed to burn.

People wouldn't want to stay in the house, then, so they would leave. However, any unpleasant forms of life that were in the house—rats, mice, bugs—might be overcome by the fumes. After the pitchy material stopped burning and the rooms had been aired out, the house would be free of these vermin. The house would have been "fumigated" (FYOO-mih-gay-ted).

Some people felt fumigation might even get rid of the evil spirits they imagined brought disease. If someone were sick and died in a house, it might be fumigated in one way or another before other people felt safe about living there.

SLAUGHTER OF A WHALE

3 The Burning of Oil

As CIVILIZATION continued to spread and grow, people needed more and more fires. There were more and more people, after all, and cities grew larger and larger. Fires were needed to keep people warm, to cook food, to make metals out of ore, pottery out of clay, glass out of sand.

Most of the time wood was used as fuel for fires. Later on, beginning in the 1600's, coal was also used. (Coal is a black solid made almost entirely of carbon atoms that were formed from buried forests hundreds of millions of years ago—but that is a different story.)

Fire was also needed for light. In the European winter, nights can be fifteen or sixteen hours long, and no one can sleep that long. Sitting awake in darkness was pretty dreary, though, so people wanted light. What's more, they wanted it where they happened to be, not just near the fireplace.

You can't carry a bonfire from place to place, but you can carry a torch, which is a piece of wood with one end soaked in oil. Or else you can use candles, made out of solid animal fat or wax. Or you can use lamps that burn vegetable oil.

As cities continued to grow, more and more lights were needed, especially when the only way to make cities safe was to light up all the streets—and keep them lit up all during the night.

Where could one get the fat and oil needed for all those lamps and torches and candles?

In the 1600's and 1700's, large whales were hunted in the oceans. They were warm-blooded animals and they had a thick layer of blubber (a kind of fat) under their skins that protected them from the cold polar seas. Huge quantities of "whale oil" could be obtained from this blubber, and it was used in lamps.

However, the whales could not last forever. It became harder and harder to find them and some kinds were almost killed off. Whaling ships had to go down to the Antarctic to find more whales, and it was clear that whale oil could not be used to feed the lamps for long.

What about coal? There seemed to be unending quantities of that underground. Coal could be heated in such a way that it would not burn. Instead, it would give off vapors called "coal gas" that could be made to burn. The coal gas could be collected, stored, and then be led through pipes until a small, steady stream of gas would come out of jets in places where light was desired. The gas coming out of the jets could be set on fire, and the yellow flame would then light up the surroundings. As long as coal gas was formed and stored, the gas jets would be "eternal flames."

The first to show that this would really work was a Scottish inventor named William Murdock. He had a

LAMPLIGHTER

factory that manufactured steam engines, and in 1803 he lit that factory with gas jets. In 1807 some London streets began to use gas-lighting, and throughout the 1800's the use spread.

Coal not only gave off coal gas when heated in a way that kept it from burning, it also gave off a black pitchy material called "coal tar." When this coal tar was heated under proper conditions, a clear liquid was given off.

This liquid is a mixture of hydrocarbons. The smaller hydrocarbons were easily vaporized, and they were driven off and discarded. They were not useful in lamps. They burned too easily and could explode. The larger hydrocarbon molecules (but not too large to be liquid) were what was wanted. They vaporized slowly and burned quietly in lamps.

This liquid from coal was called "coal oil."

Something like it could also be obtained from certain rocks called shale, which contained hydrocarbons in their pores. The rock is therefore called "oil shale." The hydrocarbons obtained from the shale were a soft solid that felt something like wax. When it was heated so as to drive off a liquid suitable for use in lamps, that liquid was called "kerosene" from a Greek word for "wax."

In the 1850's the lamps of Europe and America began to use coal oil or kerosene.

But in 1859 a railway conductor from New York State did something completely new.

His name was Edwin Laurentine Drake and he was forty years old at the time. He wondered if there might not be a still better source of fuel for lamps than coal or shale. Both coal and shale were solid materials that

WILLIAM MURDOCK
(1754-1839)

COLONEL EDWIN L. DRAKE
(1819-1880)

had to be dug out of the ground and carried here and there and broken up and treated in various ways to form a liquid.

What if one could make use of something that was already a liquid? Liquids are much more easily handled than solids, and it would probably be much cheaper to get proper fuel out of them.

Drake even had a good idea about what that liquid should be, for he had invested in the Pennsylvania Rock Oil Company. This company collected petroleum that had seeped to the ground near Titusville, Pennsylvania. This town is in the northwestern part of the state, about ninety miles north of Pittsburgh.

The company used the oil only for medicine. There was enough oil seepage for that, but there wasn't enough to supply the lamps of the nation. There might, however, be a larger supply underground.

People did sometimes dig deep underground. It was common to dig wells for fresh water. It was sometimes possible to dig particularly deep to get "brine," or very salty water, which was used to preserve food and for other purposes.

Sometimes when people dug for brine, oil came up with the brine. There were reports that this happened in China and Burma as long as two thousand years ago. When gaseous hydrocarbons came up out of the brine well, the ancient Chinese are supposed to have set it on fire. They then used the heat to evaporate the water from the brine to produce solid salt.

Drake knew about this, and he studied the methods used for drilling for brine. There were methods whereby a chisel could be pumped up and down from a cable to break the rock it struck against. Every once in a while, the chisel would be lifted out of the hole, the bits of broken rock would be removed, and the chisel would be put to work again.

Drake used methods like this to chisel sixty-nine feet under the ground at Titusville, and on August 28, 1859, he struck oil. Large quantities of oil could be pumped out of the ground; far more than could be obtained from seepages on the surface. Drake had drilled the first "oil well."

Once Drake succeeded, others flocked to the spot and began drilling for oil on their own. Northwestern Pennsylvania became the first oil field in the world, and boom towns sprang up. Drake hadn't patented his methods, however, and he wasn't a clever business man, so he didn't become rich. He died in 1880 a poor man.

FIRST OIL RUSH IN PENNSYLVANIA

People began to drill for oil elsewhere in the world. As it turned out, it was possible to find oil even where there were no seepages on the ground to give its presence away.

The oil that exists deep underground and slowly seeps upward through the pores in sedimentary rock doesn't always reach the surface. Sometimes it moves up against the lower boundary of a layer of rock that is really solid and has no pores. That stops the oil and traps it in the porous rock beneath the layer of solid rock.

If anyone can drill through that solid rock into the porous rock beneath, oil can be brought up. In fact, sometimes the oil in the porous rock is under considerable pressure from water still farther down. When the drilling penetrates the solid rocks, oil shoots upward like a fountain. This was called a "gusher."

But how could anyone tell where there was solid rock with oil-bearing porous rock underneath? This isn't easy, but there were people who carefully studied the rock formations of the ground and tried to estimate what the chances were of finding oil.

The only way to tell for sure is to drill. If there is no oil, that is a "dry well." If there *is* oil, that is good news and other areas nearby are drilled for additional oil.

New and better methods of drilling were worked out. There were special metal "bits" devised that could be turned round and round, grinding away through rock. The hole that is formed is kept full of a kind of mud that carries away the chipped rock as it collects and also keeps the oil from lifting up wildly once it is reached. (A gusher wastes a great deal of oil.)

35

A GUSHER

Nowadays there are over six hundred thousand wells producing oil all over the world—and it all started with Drake's oil well in 1859.

The oil that is obtained from oil wells has a number of uses. It can be "refined," that is, separated into different kinds of hydrocarbons. The best way of doing that is to "distill" it, that is, to heat it in such a way as to boil off and collect first the small hydrocarbon molecules, then larger ones, then still larger ones, and so on.

The large-molecule hydrocarbons are soft solids that could be used for paving. Not quite such large mole-

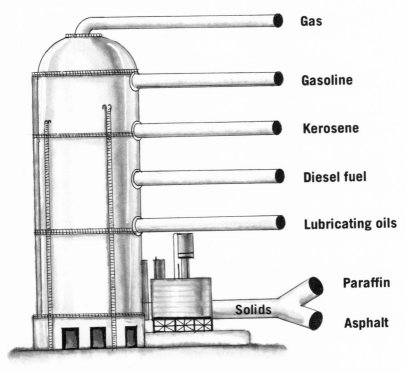

DISTILLATION OF PETROLEUM PRODUCTS

cules are liquids that could be used to lubricate machinery and keep it working smoothly. Very small molecules of "natural gas" could be used to feed the gas jets of the nation.

The most important petroleum product at the time of the first oil well consisted of middle-sized molecules. This was just like the kerosene that was used for lamps. For a few decades, kerosene lamps all over the United States, and gradually in other parts of the world, too, were fed by fuel obtained from petroleum.

There were also petroleum products with small-sized molecules, molecules larger than those of natural gas and smaller than those of kerosene. These in-between molecules were easily evaporated liquids. They were too easily evaporated to be used in kerosene lamps. They would produce so much vapor that they would explode. There was nothing to do with such small-molecule parts of petroleum except to get rid of them somehow as, for instance, by burning them.

And yet, for a time, it might have seemed that petroleum was going to drop out of fashion as quickly as it had arrived. In 1879 an American inventor, Thomas Alva Edison, invented the electric light. That was only twenty years after the first oil well had been drilled.

The electric light gave a much steadier light than either a gas jet or a kerosene lamp. What's more, an electric light didn't have an open flame like a gas jet or kerosene lamp, so the electric light wasn't as likely to start fires.

As the use of electricity became more common, electric lights grew in number and spread everywhere. Gas jets and kerosene lamps went increasingly out of use.

Now what would people need petroleum for? Would the oil wells shut down?

THOMAS EDISON AND HIS ELECTRIC BULB

**HENRY FORD
(1863-1947)**

**THOMAS EDISON
(1847-1931)**

40

4 The New Importance of Oil

ACTUALLY, something else was coming along that was far more important than kerosene lamps and gas jets.

In the 1700's, steam engines had been built. In a steam engine a fire heats water until it boils and turns into steam. The steam enters an engine and its pressure makes pistons move back and forth and wheels turn. The fire is outside the engine, so it is an "external-combustion engine."

Suppose, though, that you have a tank of inflammable liquid that easily turns into a vapor. A tiny bit of the vapor is led into the engine where it is mixed with air. A spark causes the vapor-air mixture to explode, and the force of this tiny explosion causes the pistons to move. The exploded vapor-air mixture is pushed out of the engine, more vapor is led in and mixed with air, and another tiny explosion is produced.

An endless series of tiny explosions makes the pistons move back and forth steadily. Because the fire (and an explosion is just a rapid fire) takes place *inside* the engine, the result is an "internal-combustion engine."

41

The important advantage of an internal-combustion engine is that it starts at once. A steam engine won't start until the water is heated up and comes to a boil, and that can take quite a time. A vapor-air mixture can explode at once, however, as soon as a spark is applied.

The first practical internal-combustion engine was built in 1860 by a French inventor, Etienne Lenoir (luh-NWAHR). In 1876 a better version was built by a German inventor, Nikolaus August Otto. The internal-combustion engine designed by Otto (with improvements, of course) is still the kind used today.

If the internal-combustion engine is hooked up to the wheels of a carriage in the proper way, the movement of the pistons in the engine will turn the wheels. You won't need a horse to pull the carriage. In this way, you would have a "horseless carriage." Pretty soon such a device came to be called an "automobile," from a combination of Greek and Latin words meaning "self-moving."

The first practical automobiles were built in 1885 by two German engineers, Gottlieb Daimler (DAME-ler) and Karl Benz (BENTS). They were very expensive objects at the start.

An American engineer, Henry Ford, worked out a way, however, of building automobiles in quantity, using parts that were formed so exactly that any part would fit any automobile. He then set up an "assembly line" in which the partially built automobile was carried along to workers who stayed in the same place. Each worker would do just one job over and over as identical, partly built automobiles passed before him one after the other. As the automobile passed along the assembly line by one worker after another, it came

1918 MODEL T FORD

to be more and more finished. When it reached the end of the line, it was complete.

By 1913 Henry Ford was making a thousand automobiles a day and could charge very low prices.

Improvements kept making automobiles better and easier to drive. At first, the engine had to be given its first turn by a hand crank before the exploding vapors would take hold. This took a lot of muscle and could be dangerous if the engine started before the cranker was ready.

Then, however, a storage battery was added to the car. It produced electricity by chemical means and stored it until it was needed to start the engine. Once a car had a "self-starter," anyone could drive it.

Automobiles grew more and more common during the 1920's. Millions of them were sold; tens of millions. It seemed that every American wanted an automobile. People in other countries wanted them, too.

But what was the fuel that was going to run them all? What was the vapor that would combine with the air and explode to run the engine? What about the hydrocarbons obtained from petroleum?

The middle-sized molecules of kerosene wouldn't do. They didn't vaporize easily enough. In a lamp, slow vaporization was good; it prevented an explosion. In an internal-combustion engine, however, an explosion was exactly what was wanted.

Smaller molecules than those in kerosene were needed. In fact, what was needed were those same molecules that were useless in lamps and that the oil companies had to get rid of by burning them or otherwise. Now the oil companies could sell them to automobile owners.

These small molecules made up what came to be called "gasoline" because they turned into a vapor, or gas, so easily. Sometimes gasoline was called "gas" for short, though it was a liquid and not a gas. (The British called it "petrol," which was short for petroleum, even though it only made up a fraction of petroleum.)

Airplanes were invented by the American brothers Wilbur and Orville Wright in 1903, and they were powered by internal-combustion engines, too. They needed more and more gasoline as they grew more common.

ORVILLE AND WILBUR WRIGHT, 1903

In 1892 the German engineer Rudolf Diesel (DEEZ-el) had worked out a kind of internal-combustion engine that was simpler and needed less fuel. It could use molecules larger than those of gasoline (molecules making up "diesel fuel"), and it didn't need a spark to ignite them. The mixture was just compressed and squeezed into a very small space. The compression heated the gas mixture and that heat made it explode.

A Diesel engine was heavier than an ordinary internal-combustion engine, and it worked best for large objects like trucks, buses, and ships.

By the 1930's, internal-combustion engines had become so common that petroleum was becoming more important than coal as a fuel. The oil companies began to refine the petroleum in such a way as to squeeze as much gasoline and diesel fuel out of it as possible.

Even so, when they got all the gasoline and diesel fuel out of it that they could, there were large amounts of other parts of the petroleum left over.

Some of the liquids with longer hydrocarbon molecules would burn nicely, but hardly anyone was using kerosene lamps any more. Still, these liquids could be burned to give heat rather than light. Why not heat houses with such "fuel oil."

Through the 1920's, people had been using coal in greater and greater quantities to heat houses, but fuel oil did have advantages over coal.

Coal had to be delivered and stored in the cellar, and that was a dirty job. The coal had to be shoveled into the furnace; the fire had to be started with paper and wood; it had to be fiddled with while it was burning. Eventually, ashes had to be removed.

46

RUDOLPH DIESEL
(1858-1913)

Fuel oil could be stored underground. It could be fed to a furnace automatically and started and stopped automatically by a thermostat. There were no ashes.

Everyone who could changed from coal to oil.

The very small molecules of natural gas could also be used in jets to cook food, and in furnaces to heat houses. In some ways, natural gas was even more convenient than liquid fuels. It was cleaner and simpler to use.

The left-over hydrocarbons in petroleum were used by chemists who rearranged the atoms and added others so as to form plastics, synthetic fibers, medicines, dyes, and many other useful products.

5 The Future of Oil

THERE WAS one important question. As more and more people began to use all the different portions of petroleum for more and more purposes, how long would the oil last?

For a while in the 1930's, people thought that the oil would soon run out, but the oil companies looked everywhere to find new wells. They had learned better ways of looking, drilling, and finding.

In the late 1940's they began to find new sources of oil in the Middle East, where oil seepages and pitch had been used in the days of the earliest civilizations.

All around the Persian Gulf, rich supplies of oil existed underground. There seemed to be as much oil in the Middle East as in all the rest of the world. All at once the world supply of oil was doubled.

For a quarter of a century, oil was plentiful and cheap. The United States had its own supplies, of course, but it felt more confident about using them when it knew it could always get more from abroad. Europe and Japan, which had no oil supply of their

Greenland

Asia

Europe

North America

Africa

South America

Australia

THE WORLD'S MAJOR OIL FIELDS

own, imported oil and began to make use of its cheapness and convenience.

The situation was simple at first because, immediately after World War II, many of the oil-producing regions of the Middle East were under the control of the European nations. It was Europeans and Americans who drilled the new oil wells, owned them, and ran them.

But then the nations of the Middle East became independent. They wanted to control their own oil wells and sell it at their own prices. In 1960 the oil-producing nations of the Middle East and elsewhere formed a group called the Organization of Petroleum Exporting Countries, or OPEC for short. They began to consult with each other and to decide what prices to charge. Very soon it began to appear that OPEC was extremely powerful. The industrial nations of the world needed oil desperately. Their use of oil had gone up every year, and their industries ran on oil. So did their automobiles and trucks and buses and ships and planes. It was hard to give that up, or even cut it down, without upsetting the whole economy of the world.

Yet it seemed the amount of oil used would have to be cut down because, even with the new discoveries after World War II, the oil supply would not last long.

Some people estimate that the total amount of oil in the oil wells of the world amounts to 600 billion barrels. That is a lot of oil, but the world is consuming about 20 billion barrels of oil every year. At that rate, the oil supply will only last thirty years more.

Of course, there is still the possibility of more discoveries. A new oil field was found in northern Alaska in the late 1960's. Oil was discovered under the North Sea near Great Britain. There seems to be a great deal of oil in southern Mexico.

Still, even if we count all we are likely to discover, it doesn't seem that the oil will last more than fifty years at the rate we're using it.

What's more, the old sources are definitely drying up. The United States was the largest producer of oil for over a hundred years after Drake drilled the first oil well in Pennsylvania. The Pennsylvania fields were long since used up, but new and larger fields were discovered in Texas and elsewhere.

Now, however, all the American oil fields are dwindling. Production reached a maximum in the early 1970's, and now it is going down year by year.

Even as late as 1969, the United States produced all

BIG TEXAS REFINERY

the oil it needed for itself. Then it had to begin importing oil from abroad because it was producing less each year and because the American people were using more each year. By 1973, ten percent of the oil Americans used came from abroad. By 1980, fifty percent of the oil Americans use will come from abroad.

When the supply of oil from abroad is cut, Americans are in trouble. They begin to find it difficult to get gasoline for their automobiles and diesel fuel for the trucks and farm machinery. They have trouble getting fuel oil to heat their houses in the winter.

In 1973 the Middle Eastern countries stopped sending oil to the United States and Europe for a few months because of political disputes over the nation of Israel. Those were months of confusion. Then, in 1979, there was a revolution in Iran, a large oil-producing nation, and its production was cut down. Again confusion.

The OPEC nations argue that oil supplies can't last forever. As long as oil is cheap and plentiful, there is no feeling that anything else ought to be found as a source for energy. The nations just keep burning the oil, and in the end there will be disaster.

If the price of oil is raised and the amount produced is limited, people will be more careful about how they use the oil. They will economize and use less so the oil will last longer. Furthermore, if oil is expensive and hard to get, the nations will try harder to find new kinds of energy.

Since 1973, the OPEC nations have been raising the price of oil steadily, and that has caused the price of everything to go up, too. Now the people of the world can see that there is an energy problem and that they must begin to work on it.

But what can be done?

We have to give ourselves as much time as possible to find new sources of energy. That means we must conserve oil as much as we can. We must cut out waste. We must save.

People must buy smaller cars that can go longer distances on each gallon of gasoline. They must share rides. They must use public transportation. They must walk more. They must insulate their homes. They must get used to less heating in the winter and less air conditioning in the summer. They must travel less and take vacations closer to home.

A particularly important way of saving is to control the population. Every person uses energy, and the more people there are, the more energy is demanded. Right now there are over four billion people on earth, twice as many as there were fifty years ago, and the population is still going up. There may be six billion people on earth in the year 2000. Every effort must be made to keep the population from growing too rapidly.

Another important way of conserving energy is to work for world peace. A war is incredibly expensive in terms of energy. Even supporting an army and navy and air force without ever using them consumes fearful amounts of energy.

Then, too, oil wells are not the only source of oil, though they are the cheapest and most convenient sources. There is the shale from which kerosene was obtained over a century ago. We can go back to that.

To be sure, it is troublesome to dig up the shale; it takes energy and time and trouble to get the hydrocarbons out of it. Then we have to figure out what to do with the spent shale that's left over. Still, if we can

**VOLKSWAGEN RABBIT DIESEL
42 MILES PER GALLON**

**ROLLS ROYCE
10 MILES PER GALLON**

solve these problems, the shale would be a large source of oil. There are also "tar sands" in Canada that can be made to yield oil.

If we can use these sources, we might have oil for a hundred years.

We can even go back to coal. Coal is much more plentiful than oil, and it can be used in place of oil for many purposes. Coal can be treated chemically in such a way that some of it can be converted into liquid fuels. Such liquid fuels are sometimes called synthetic fuels. Coal could last for a number of centuries.

One difficulty is that both coal and oil, when burned, tend to pollute the atmosphere with smoke containing irritating and harmful chemicals that arise from the small amounts of impurities present.

Even if such impurities are removed, burning coal and oil produce carbon dioxide that accumulates in the air. Carbon dioxide in the air tends to trap sunlight and warm the earth. Even a little carbon dioxide in the air might change the planet's climate, and this could create enormous problems.

We must therefore find energy sources other than coal and oil that do not have these dangers. We could use the energy of the wind, of running water, of wood and vegetation, of tides, of ocean waves, of the heat inside the earth. All of this probably isn't enough for our needs, but if we learn to use them efficiently, we will help keep ourselves going until we can find something better still.

We can use altogether new sources of energy. We have been using nuclear energy from uranium fission, for instance, but many people fear that this is too dangerous to use. It might spread radioactivity over the earth. A different kind of nuclear energy is hydrogen fusion, which would supply more and cheaper energy than uranium fission does. It would do so, scientists believe, more safely. The trouble is that we haven't quite figured out how to make hydrogen fusion work in such a way as to yield energy.

Another source is the sun itself. There is enough sunlight striking the earth and going to waste to supply us with all the energy we can possibly need. We will have to work out ways to collect some of that sunlight and use it.

It is possible that we might set up collecting stations in space, orbiting about the earth. Such stations would beam the energy down to the earth in the form of short radio waves called "microwaves." The microwaves could then be turned into electricity.

There are many things we could do to keep ourselves going as the oil wells run dry. We have to keep our wits about us, though. We have to cooperate the whole world over and we have to work hard and fast.

SOLAR ENERGY COLLECTOR IN ORBIT

Index